ROLE-PLAYING FOR FUN AND PROFIT™

HAUNTED HOUSES

JEANNE NAGLE

rosen publishing's
rosen
central®

New York

For Laura. "Halloween!"

Published in 2016 by The Rosen Publishing Group, Inc.
29 East 21st Street, New York, NY 10010

Library of Congress Cataloging-in-Publication Data

Nagle, Jeanne.
Haunted houses Jeanne Nagle. —First edition.
    pages cm.—(Role-playing for fun and profit)
Includes bibliographical references and index.
ISBN 978-1-4994-3718-8 (library bound)—
ISBN 978-1-4994-3716-4 (pbk.)—ISBN 978-1-4994-3717-1 (6-pack)
1. Haunted houses—Juvenile literature. 2. Ghosts—Juvenile literature. 3. Role playing—
Juvenile literature I. Title.
BF1475.N34 2015
793.9—dc23
2015022786

Manufactured in the United States of America

CONTENTS

A private home in Santa Barbara, California, stands decorated for Halloween. The spirit of the season, in attractions great and small, creates a need for haunted-house workers.

For many people, haunted houses are little more than a scary treat they indulge in around Halloween. They wait in long lines and pay for the privilege of being scared half to death. Others see haunted attractions as hotbeds of opportunity that can benefit them all year round. The second group are not paying customers looking for a few fall thrills. They are career-minded individuals with a desire to practice work skills in their chosen field, making haunted houses part of a serious effort to carve out a career path for themselves.

A house with darkened rooms filled with assorted ghouls and buckets of blood may not seem like an ideal work training ground. But brush aside the cobwebs and peek behind that wall of chainsaws, and a professional business, with all types of employees, will appear. (Heck, simply forking over cash for an entry ticket should be a giant clue that every chamber of horrors is designed to be a money-making venture.)

So are the folks jumping out at haunted house customers planning to become professional monsters or the working undead? Maybe, but more likely they are actors—or wannabe actors—who play these roles to get useful experience. They get plenty of help from makeup, hair, and costume designers, some of who also may be learning their craft and getting a start in their fields through jobs at a haunted attraction. It's a safe bet that a number of light and sound technicians, as well as special effects masters, have begun their careers creating sights and sounds that give haunted-house visitors the heebie-jeebies.

People who prefer to work in a more traditional field and setting, such as an office, can gain experience in this way. After all, somebody has to run the business end of haunted attractions. From management and marketing to production and employee payroll, a typical professional haunted house has a position for just about everyone.

Even if there isn't a professional attraction nearby, people can still get experience by working at a haunted house. Large-scale productions are not the only game in this ghost town. Each Halloween season, hundreds of haunted houses and scary hayrides crop up in towns and cities across the United States. Some are created to raise funds for charities while others are a seasonal side business for established companies and organizations. Still others are built mainly by people who just like to have fun. Each and every one of these smaller haunted attractions needs workers, just like the big name-brand offerings.

Finding, getting, and keeping a job as part of a haunted house's cast or crew takes talent, of course. But it also takes hard work. Gaining hands-on experience that can be used in a rewarding job field is well worth the effort.

CHAPTER ONE

SCARE TACTICS

Not knowing what might happen next is part of the thrill of going through a haunted attraction. People expect to be tense and surprised in such a situation. Being caught off guard is not a good way to get a job, however. Experts recommend that job seekers learn everything they can about the industry—even a specific company or organization—they would like to join.

Learning as much as possible about the business is the first step toward success as a haunted attraction employee. Important points to consider include the types of attractions that might be looking for help, how such operations are run, and what is needed for them to stay in business.

TYPES OF HAUNTED ATTRACTIONS

Classic haunted houses are the most common, and possibly the most popular, type of haunted attractions in North America. These are actual houses or buildings with several rooms in

Haunted houses are filled with scary sights and strange creatures. What goes on inside such places should be shocking, not working inside them.

them. It is dark inside, and all sorts of creepy things appear or happen to anyone who enters. Most often people walk (or run, if they are scared) through haunted houses. Riding in cars that roll along specially built tracks is an option for those who visit haunted attractions set up in amusement parks.

Open-air riding is available with another kind of attraction, the haunted hayride. This is a nighttime activity that takes place in wooded areas or on farms. Passengers sit on bales of hay or straw in wagons pulled by a tractor, truck, or, rarely, horses. Scary sights are everywhere, and passengers never know when someone—or something—will jump out at them from behind

HAUNT HISTORY

Some people trace the history of haunted attractions—sometimes called simply "haunts" for short—back to ancient Egypt. Dead kings and queens were placed in tombs that featured all sorts of tricks and scary objects designed to keep thieves from stealing treasures buried with the royals. Secret passages, mazes, booby traps, and drawings or carvings of fierce beasts were all designed to scare anybody who entered a tomb.

Modern haunts are connected with traveling carnivals and fairs. Early "ghost houses" were usually buildings that people could walk through in the dark. A little later, carts on tracks were added so people could ride through haunts. These "ghost trains" were very popular in the early twentieth century.

A young couple ride a 1960s ghost train at an amusement park in Belle Harbour, New York.

a tree. Some haunted hayrides also feature eerie music and sound effects.

People also go into the woods when they choose to walk a haunted trail. The setting and surprises for this type of haunted attraction are the same as those for haunted hayrides. The difference is that visitors wind their way through about a mile of scares on foot. This puts them in closer contact with all the frightening action, making it more like a haunted house experience than a hayride. A number of farms cut twisting, turning paths through their cornfields to make a haunted maze. This is a lot like a haunted trail, with surprises appearing suddenly out from corn stalks instead of trees in a forest or wood.

EXTRA-SPECIAL SPOOKINESS

While trying to gain more of an audience, and give themselves an edge over the competition, haunt operators have gone beyond simply houses, hayrides, and trails. New and creative ways to scare people are an important part of the haunted attraction business.

Putting a scary spin on existing events is one way new haunted attractions are born. Scavenger hunts, where teams visit many local spots in search of special objects, is one such event. Haunted scavenger hunts can be for the whole family or for adults only. The National Gallery of Art in Washington, DC, has had both. During the 2012 Halloween season, the gallery hosted a wizard-themed hunt one day for children ages nine through twelve. Then, a week later, those eighteen and over were invited to seek and photograph skeletons and cut-off body parts that could be found throughout the gallery's buildings.

Road rallies, which are basically scavenger hunts using a car or other vehicle, also get otherwordly treatment. A road rally is a race where teams drive following cluelike directions, trying to make it to different points around the course by a specific time. The Danger Run in Louisville, Kentucky, has been a favorite haunted attraction of this kind for more than twenty years. Participants follow clues that lead them to two or three haunted houses in the Louisville area. Teams do not try to beat the clock so much as not get lost so they can make it to all the haunts before closing time.

There is also a new twist on haunted houses that makes visitors part of the attraction. Over the past few years, haunted theater has become popular in and around the city of Los Angeles. This type of attraction combines live theater, haunted houses, and audience participation. Attractions such as *Delusion*, which has called itself the first "haunted play," follow a plot or storyline and have visitors interact with the characters. Because horror theater attractions are based in big cities— where movies and television shows are taped and professional plays are produced—visitors can expect awesome stunts and special effects during these shows.

WHERE GOBLINS LIVE

Haunts take place at various locations, depending on the type of attraction one is visiting. Even though they are called haunted houses, these attractions do not necessarily take place in an actual house. Barns, warehouses, nightclubs, and office buildings are

Some classic haunts resemble seemingly normal houses. A place that looks like California's Winchester Mystery House, supposedly haunted by a former owner, would work well in the haunt market.

also popular haunt spots. Attraction owners like to use abandoned buildings if possible because they are cheaper to rent. Also, a place that is no longer actively used tends to look run-down and creepier.

Building a haunted house from scratch may be necessary if an existing location is not available. Even within existing buildings, there is generally some construction work to do. For instance, walls could be put in a warehouse to create various rooms and hallways, making the attraction "feel" like a real house. Indoor mazes are also created using building materials such as plywood and sheets of plastic.

ROOM FOR A THRILL

Small, "homemade" haunted attractions, meaning haunted houses that the neighbors might run on Halloween, usually show off an assortment of scary stuff throughout the site. Professional haunts, however, are likely to have a theme or themes that tie everything together. Sometimes there is a main theme. The Dent Schoolhouse in Cincinnati uses a story about missing students to adopt a haunted school theme.

The most popular and easiest way to incorporate a theme, however, is by using theme rooms in a haunted house and various areas in hayride and trail attractions. Each room has characters and props focused on a specific idea or situation. In one room visitors might see a crazy doctor with bloody body parts, and in the next there might be evil clowns. The Dent Schoolhouse builds on its overall school theme to feature rooms such as an auto shop and auditorium set up for the prom that are designed to appear haunted in a room-specific way.

A creepy clown poses for a photo in the halls of a Virginia haunted house. Such characters are popping up in less-traditional haunt types and locations as well.

A theater marquee advertising a séance with dead magician Harry Houdini sets the stage for frightening activities at "Knott's Scary Farm" in California.

MACABRE MAKEOVERS

Amusement parks frequently make room on their grounds for haunted attractions during the Halloween season. Knott's Berry Farm in California is famous for turning the entire theme park into a giant haunt called "Knott's Scary Farm." The regular rides are given a spooky makeover, workers are dressed like creepy characters, and the whole park is divided into "scare zones." Other organizations and tourist spots such as museums turn all or part of their headquarters into haunts in the fall.

FRIGHTENINGLY ORGANIZED

Haunted attractions are subject to the same rules and policies that any other business or event has to follow. Owners must file for and receive a permit from the city, town, county, or province in which they are located. A permit is legal permission to charge money for an event or attraction. This is true whether the haunt is designed to make money for charity or provide cash to the owner/operator.

Applications for permits require basic information such as the name and contact information of the operator, dates and times when the haunt will be open to the public, and a description, usually with sketches, of the attraction. Haunts also need to meet certain requirements. For one thing, attractions must meet all safety and local, state, and federal laws. Another requirement is adequate parking and restrooms for guests and employees. Haunts should scare visitors but not annoy their neighbors with loud noises, especially not early in the morning or late at night.

Once a fee has been paid and the permit given, haunts are free to prepare for their opening. This is the time when attraction owners start hiring for jobs that can give people experience in the career field of their dreams.

CHAPTER TWO

GHOULS OF THE TRADE

Unlike ghosts, large and professional haunted attractions do not suddenly appear out of thin air. Plenty of planning goes into getting a haunt up and running. Even though most attractions are open for only a couple of months in the fall, the work that goes into their creation can be a year-round thing. What's more, many real, live people are responsible for creating these haunted worlds, as well as bringing to life the creatures that make visitors' hearts race. Owners/operators, business staff, and cast members make it their business to haunt people's dreams.

STARTING THE SHOW

Chances are that anyone who owns and runs a haunted attraction looked forward to Halloween as a child. In fact, owners never really outgrew that feeling of excitement when fall rolls around and pumpkins start getting carved. Gory stuff, scaring people, and being scared themselves hold a special place in the hearts of those who make a living through haunts.

Beyond simply handing out frights, haunted attraction owners want to entertain people. Haunts are actually special shows or plays that use thrills and chills to tell a story. Running a haunt, then, makes the owner the director, the one who has the idea of how the story should be told and makes it happen by giving directions. He or she is also like a theater producer, who arranges to get the money the show needs. Finally, haunt owners are businesspeople who lead a staff of professionals and try to make a living putting on their show.

The owners of the Screemers complex of haunted attractions in Toronto give bonuses to employees, such as this chainsaw maniac character, who make guests wet their pants with fright.

HAUNTED BY DETAILS

Haunt owners have many responsibilities. As mentioned, the first few include finding a building or site to use and getting all the permits in order. The next step is getting the money to get the attraction ready for the public. This includes paying rent on a building or land, buying supplies, renting or buying props and special effects equipment, and paying all the people who work

TIME AND MONEY

Haunted attractions are a booming business in North America. A 2011 report posted on the website Business Unusual (www. businessunusual.net) estimates that haunts are responsible for pumping $400 to $500 million into the economy. That's pretty good for any industry, but keep in mind that most haunts usually operate for only three to five months each year.

Still, it can be difficult to become wealthy, or even pay the bills, being a haunted attraction owner and operator. It can take years before the owners of larger haunts make back the money they invested in their operations, let alone turn a profit or make money beyond what they originally spent.

Anyone who wants to open a haunted attraction needs to have a rough idea in mind about what they want to create. This includes figuring out how big the attraction should be, a theme or storyline, the kinds of equipment and materials needed, and the time frame needed to make the attraction a reality.

for them. Electricity and water bills also have to be included in the budget.

If haunts have been operating for a few years, they may be able to pay for themselves . . . eventually. Yet many owners find it necessary to take out business loans from banks, especially when they first open.

WHAT IT TAKES TO BE THE BOSS

Owners are playful and creative people for sure. But first and foremost, they must also be businesspeople. In a 2005 Associated Press interview, Leonard Pickel, the editor of *Haunted Attractions* magazine, stressed this point. "So many people who get in the business are artist-types who enjoy scaring people and don't understand that if you don't have the money, you don't get to play anymore," Pickel said. "Scaring people is easy. Making money scaring people is a lot harder."

Anybody hoping to own or run a haunted attraction would be smart to start out working in the business office of an independent haunt or amusement park that has a haunted attraction. Future owners might start out working under an owner in operations, which is the department that makes sure everything is running smoothly and according to plan. Marketing and advertising is another business area that beginners might want to investigate. These types of jobs involve making sure the public knows about the haunted house. They also hype how great the attraction is so that as many people as possible visit, and they oversee the selling of tickets.

SCARY STORIES

In a way, haunts are like ghost stories that come to life. Not only do attractions have themes or theme rooms, but some of them have an entire back story. These stories include details and made-up facts about the haunt that build anticipation in the minds of haunted attraction customers. The more background—about who or what lives there, reasons for the action that is taking place, how the location became haunted to begin with—the better the experience will be for visitors.

Owners, who have put a lot of thought into their haunt right from the get-go, like to help write the story, known as a script. Professional writers, known as scriptwriters, can also be hired to create a back story. Companies such as Hauntrepreneurs in Texas and Imaginarts Studios in New York State have scriptwriters working for them as part of their design team. Smaller haunts may be willing to work with new writers who are looking to gain experience in the field.

PLAYING A MONSTER ROLE

Since haunted attractions are very much like plays and shows, people use some of the same words to describe theater jobs when talking about haunt employment. For instance, a group of actors who are in a play together are called a cast. The same is true for actors pretending to be characters at a haunted attraction. (That is why when someone is looking to hire actors for a haunted house they may refer to it as a "casting call.")

An actor, in character as a demented carnival worker, waits to welcome guests to a haunt in Maine.

An actor's job is to look, talk, and act like a certain type of character. Haunt actors behave like creatures that either do not exist or are taken to the extreme. Examples include make-believe monsters and human beings who are totally crazy or evil, such as mad scientists or serial killers. Owners can give actors an idea of how they should play their characters. Writers set up a storyline and even give actors lines to say. Yet each actor is also responsible for adding bits and pieces of their own performance.

Because they are the ones who have the strongest connection to, and make the biggest impression on, paying cus-

The cast of a haunted attraction in Salem, Massachusetts, gathers for a group photo inside Dracula's Castle. Actors take their cues from writers and haunt themes to develop their characters.

tomers, actors are very important to the success of a haunt. "You can put in all the bells and whistles, but if you don't have great actors, it doesn't work," says longtime haunted attraction owner Steve Kopelman. "It's the actors that bring people into the haunted house, so you really need good actors to carry off everything."

SKILLS AND EXPERIENCE

Once a haunt actor has landed a job, he or she also has to rehearse, or practice, the role. Actors rehearse on their own, but more important, they have to rehearse with other cast members as well.

Unlike actors in a play, who say their lines once and move on to the rest of the play, haunt cast members perform several times each night. Every visitor to their haunt deserves and gets the full fright treatment. With hundreds, maybe thousands of paying guests going through an attraction each shift—and each shift lasting between five and seven hours—actors must stay in character a long time. Being able to repeat actions and lines, which are words they are supposed to say while in character, takes concentration and a good memory.

Playing a part in a haunted attraction is hard work physically. Actors in these situations spend almost all their time walking, standing, running, and jumping. Some characters wear hot, heavy costumes, and most wear masks or layers of makeup. These things can make a person very uncomfortable, or even cause injury. Being as fit as possible is a good thing in this business.

The best way to plan ahead for a job like this is to have some acting or theater work under one's belt. Middle schoolers and high school students should join theater clubs and participate in school plays. Towns and cities also offer community theater companies, where anyone who lives in the area can try out for a part in a play. Classes in acting and movement also look good on a haunted-attraction application for this type of work.

CHAPTER THREE

WEAPONS AND WHATNOT

The scene is straight out of somebody's worst nightmare. Flaming torches light a path that leads up to a door covered in dust and cobwebs. Inside, the walls are spattered with blood, and creepy organ music mixes with hair-raising screams that don't sound human. A man with scars all over his face welcomes visitors who dare enter. He would shake hands, but that is hard to do while holding an ax in one hand and a cut-off head in the other.

Traveling through the twisting, turning hallways of the haunted house is hard because it is dark. A green glow coming from some rooms and occasional lightning flashes help a little, though. There is enough light to see people run away from a woman zombie, only to be stopped dead in their tracks by a giant robot spider.

Visitors may never see a haunted attraction's tech crew members, but they sure do enjoy what these employees do. These workers include set and costume designers, makeup artists, and special-effects "wizards."

Items such as this scarecrow, standing guard in front of a haunted corn maze in Colorado, generally are the work of set designers and prop masters.

ALL SET

Each haunt has its own sets and props. Creating a set involves making a space look like a certain location using painted images or decorations. Props are objects that would naturally be found in a certain setting. Each room or scary scene in a haunt is a set. All the items on a haunt set, from furniture to paintings on the walls or books on a table—or fake body parts—are props.

Set designers for haunted attractions follow a script or story as they work. Their job is to make an attraction look like wherever the story takes place. It could be a crazy doctor's lab, a dungeon (which is like a jail), or some other place where spooky stuff happens. Sometimes, haunts are supposed to look like regular places where something has gone very wrong. For instance, the Haunted School House attraction in Akron, Ohio, is built in a real old school building. It has classrooms and an auditorium. Each year set designers turn these and the rest of the attraction's rooms into haunted versions of themselves.

Every haunt set designer knows that it is not enough just to slap some paint on the walls and jam various pieces of furniture into a room. These workers take the time to create scenes that are like art. To create the right mood and get the best scares, they build elaborate sets and add eye-catching props.

HIRED BY DESIGN

Haunted attractions manage to keep set-design crews busy. Some even hire design and building crews year-round, with people starting construction and setting up next year's haunt right after breaking down (taking apart and storing pieces of) the current year's version. So the good news for anyone hoping to get experience working as a haunt set designer is that there are jobs to be had in this field.

Those with training and experience have an edge over other applicants for set-design jobs. The training part comes by taking classes in art, especially drawing and sculpting. Classes can focus on art that is created by hand, work that is made using computer programs, or some combination of the two. Learning about the history of plays and theater, through English classes

Guests admire the lights and fog outside a haunted house in Southern California. Several elements come together to set the mood for a good haunt.

or drama club, would not hurt either.

Many times a person can learn about design not only by reading or hearing a lecture but by actually "doing" design. Participating in an industrial arts program, sometimes known as shop class, is a great example of training combined with actual experience. Informal training, meaning learning outside of school, and experience can also come from hobbies such as building models from one's imagination, not a packaged kit.

As with actors, gaining experience in school or community theater productions is a plus. Volunteering to use a paintbrush, swing a hammer, and locate or build props can lead to a paying job building and designing sets for one's favorite haunt. Set designers can then keep working on individual haunts or get a job with a company that designs haunted houses for other people. Experience with haunted attractions can also lead workers to paying jobs in professional theater or other design-related jobs, such as exhibit displays in museums or stores.

HELPING ACTORS LOOK LIKE DEATH

If an actor with a freshly washed face and dressed in regular clothes jumped out from the darkness of a haunted house, people might be startled, but they would not be scared. Even the best actors need help getting into their characters. Haunted attractions hire people to apply makeup that makes actors appear as if they walked straight out of a horror movie. Costume designers put together outfits that emphasize actors' roles and add to the creepiness of their characters.

Makeup artists are basically in charge of making humans into special effects. They do this by applying foundation and other cosmetics. These are not typical types of makeup that can be bought at a drug store or even a costume shop. Haunt makeup workers use the same grade of makeup that theater, television, and movie actors wear. These products are generally thick, heavy, and designed to stay on for a long time no matter what an actor goes through. The tools that makeup designers use include sponges and brushes. Airbrushing, where a machine sprays on a light coat of makeup, is also increasingly being used by haunted attractions.

At the professional haunt level, they also work with prosthetics, meaning masks and other fake features that change the shape of a person's face or body. Prosthetics are made out of chemically produced materials such as latex and silicone. Makeup artists keep prosthetics in place using a special glue. They put on makeup over the prosthetic and the actor's skin so that the fake pieces blend in with real skin.

Costume designers create clothing that fits not only an actor's body but also the appearance and style of his or her character. Some of the costumes are put together using various pieces of clothing that are already made. Others are designed by the costumer and made from scratch. Making costumes means buying fabric, cutting, and sewing.

MAKEUP AND COSTUME REQUIREMENTS

Both makeup artists and costume designers combine research and imagination to make their crafts work. Research is necessary when the action in a haunt or room takes place in the past or in a location not familiar to many people. Styling scenes so that they are at least pretty accurate helps make them more believable. Imagination lets makeup artists and costume designers give extra flair to the strange situations and gruesome characters. Also, because there may not be a lot of money available, especially for costumes, these workers need to find inexpensive ways to do their jobs.

Haunts would much prefer that their makeup and costume people not be total amateurs. In other words, they would rather hire someone with experience to handle jobs such as these,

An actor gets an airbrush touch-up from one of a Colorado haunt's makeup artists. Paint and prosthetics help define a character's mindset and attitude.

which are so visible and important to an attraction's success. Doing hair and makeup for any event—from being on the crew of a school play or simply helping a friend get ready for the prom—is a start. The same goes for costume designers. The closer someone comes to doing the type of makeup or costumes used for haunted attractions, however, the better. Either way, the person doing the styling should record their work by taking pictures or a video of the finished product.

TECH EFFECTS

Haunted attraction technical workers, called the "tech crew" for short, operate all of a haunt's electrical and technology-based

TAKING HAUNTS PERSONALLY

Technology has become a huge part of the haunt industry. One of the newest tech advances to be used in haunted attractions is radio-frequency identification (RFID) tags. These devices make it so that each fright can be personalized.

A haunted attraction called the Nest in Arizona claims to be the first haunt to use RFID technology. Nest visitors who agree to get a personalized trip through the haunt are given a badge with an RFID chip attached before they enter. RFID readers, placed in various spots throughout the attraction, use a special code on the badge to identify and track visitors. Actors check monitors linked to the readers, which allows them to call people by name as they walk—or run—past the actor's position.

Visitors also have the option to link to their Facebook accounts. Information and pictures from a visitor's account are then used to personalize the scare. For instance, someone's name suddenly may appear on a graveyard headstone, or a picture of them and their friends turns into the image of horrible zombies.

effects. That includes lighting and sound effects as well as computerized creatures and props.

After talking to the owner/scriptwriter, the leader of the tech crew decides how much and what type of effects to use, as well as where lights and speakers should be placed. Tech crews are also in charge of installation, which means actually putting all the equipment in place and wiring it so that it works.

In addition to lights and sound, many haunted attractions use animatronics. These are electronic and mechanical figures, like robots. The tech crew also installs and operates these items. Very experienced crew members may also invent and build animatronic creatures. Also controlled by the tech crew are visual effects such as DVD images projected on a wall or window.

WHO CAN CREW?

First and foremost, tech crew members need to be familiar with and able to operate special-effects equipment. Some tasks a person might be able to learn on the job. But the really complicated stuff, such as programming and wiring, is better left to the professionals. Getting at least some training, through tech workshops or computer classes at school, can help haunt workers better understand how the haunt's lights, sounds, and animatronics work.

Again, theater is a great training ground for this type of job. Joining a play's stage crew lets students learn how to operate a theater light board and create sound effects off stage.

CHAPTER FOUR

BECOMING A HAUNTER

Working for a haunted attraction is certainly different from working at a fast-food restaurant, mowing lawns, or answering phones in someone's office. Yet the way in which a person goes about finding and getting a haunt job is pretty much the same as it is in other fields. Anyone who hopes to make a career out of haunting, or simply wants to gain experience by doing a job that haunters do (acting, costuming, set design, etc.), needs to first search and apply for haunted attraction jobs. Applicants should be able to show that they meet all the requirements of the job. Haunt employers want to see proof of each applicant's experience and talent through portfolios and auditions.

The process does not stop once someone has landed a job at a haunted house or similar attraction. Keeping such a job means that the employee be dedicated, dependable, and professional.

One actor touches up the color of another's hair before work. Pitching in wherever and whenever needed is the mark of a dedicated haunt employee. .

STARTING THE SEARCH

Much like haunts themselves, job searches—in any and every field—have become strongly technology-based. People looking for work can go to a company's website, look for the "employment" or "careers" page, and browse through (look over) the positions that are available. Haunts post work openings on their websites and offer the option to apply online as well.

Job search sites such as Monster (www.monster.com) and Indeed (www.indeed.com) are other resources that people can use to find work in their field. This method is useful if a job seeker is not sure which haunts are nearby or which of those are actually hiring workers in their area of interest. Searchers simply key in the type of job they are looking for and the location where they want to work, and the search engine does the rest. This method is a little less direct than going to a haunted attraction's website. Future haunters need to figure out which search terms will bring

Big-name employers such as Disneyland, whose haunted holiday mansion is promoted here, might advertise for worker openings or hire from within.

up the most and best results. Putting the words "haunted house" into the search field of these sites will bring all sorts of haunted attraction jobs, not just the particular type of haunt job a person seeks. But entering "actor" will result in acting jobs in all sorts of fields, not just haunts. Finding the right position in the right field can be done. It just might take a little more time than going to a haunt's site directly.

When it comes to finding haunted attraction jobs, people can also go to the source. That means finding a haunt in the area and contacting the business office directly—in person or by phone—to see if there are positions available. Filling out an application on the spot and handing it right to someone could get it noticed sooner.

AUDITIONS AND PORTFOLIOS

Once a haunted job hunter's application has been accepted, he or she hopefully will be called in for an interview. This is the time when applicants talk about their work experience and share personal qualities that would make them good employees. It is also a chance for job seekers to show what they can do. Actors prove themselves through auditions. Those who want to become haunt makeup artists, costumers, or set designers should bring a portfolio with them to the interview.

Auditions show people how well someone can act. Performing a short scene from a play is one way to audition. Some haunts might hold group auditions, where groups of actors are told to move a certain way or act like a

DIGITAL PORTFOLIOS

Years ago, job seekers used to bring "hard copy" samples of their work with them to interviews. Going along with today's online job searches and applications, however, more people are using digital, or electronic, portfolios.

A digital portfolio is a multimedia presentation of work samples. In addition to drawings and photographs, digital portfolios can include video, sound, and music. Simple versions are like website pages, where multimedia information can be placed in separate sections. More complicated digital portfolios sometimes look and feel like movie trailers online.

There are several services that can help someone create a digital portfolio of their own. Google Sites (https://accounts.google.com), Dropr (http://www.dropr.com), and Silk (http://www.silk.co) are three digital portfolio-building sites recommended on the Free Technology for Teachers blog (http://www.freetech4teachers.com).

particular kind of character. Those in charge of hiring choose the actors who are most believable when doing these things.

Instead of auditioning as actors do, people who seek other types of creative jobs with haunts show a portfolio of their past work. A portfolio is made up of work samples that back up a person's claim that he or she can do a certain job. Pictures of haunt creatures in full makeup, being applied by an applicant, are portfolio worthy. A set designer's portfolio might contain drawings of a haunt set before it is built or photographs of the finished set. Costume designers should show drawings and pictures of their work, or they could even include all or part of an actual costume.

Showing pieces of work that all look alike, or even exactly the same—no matter how good that work is—will bore an employer rather than impress him or her. The best portfolios include a mix of samples showing various styles of work.

OTHER HAUNTER CONSIDERATIONS

People of any age can work at a haunted house they or their friends might build in their neighborhood. To work at a professional haunt, though, there are usually age requirements. Amusement parks have been known to hire workers as young as fifteen, but sixteen is usually the minimum age for most haunted attractions. Some places prefer that haunters be at least eighteen years old. Because they deal with the public, including younger children, haunters also might have to go through a background check and drug testing.

Haunted attraction workers must be willing and able to work nights and weekends. But there is a time commitment beyond those working hours when a person agrees to work at a haunt. In the weeks leading up to the haunt opening, workers need to be on site, either building sets, working in the office, or attending rehearsals.

As with any job, haunted attraction workers need to be on time and work whenever they are scheduled during the season. Haunt owners count on their employees to pull off the big scare, so workers need to be dependable. Finally, haunters must love

The haunted attraction Dante's Inferno at New York's famous Coney Island is shown here. Amusement parks are generally more willing to hire teens to work at their haunted attractions.

what they do and bring that enthusiasm and energy to work with them every night. With a little talent and a great attitude, anyone can be a successful haunter—and there's no telling where that first haunt job might lead.

GLOSSARY

amateur A person who does not have much experience at doing something, or who performs a job or task as a volunteer, not as a paying job.

animatronics Puppets or robots that electronically come to life.

anticipation The state of expecting something will happen.

attraction An interesting or entertaining place or event that people are excited about taking part in or visiting.

audition A brief performance meant to show how talented someone is.

character A person or thing that is part of a play or show, which an actor brings to life.

enthusiasm Great interest or excitement.

ghoul An evil, nonhuman being.

interaction When two or more people or creatures share an experience together.

portfolio A grouping of work that proves a person's experience and skill level.

prop An object that is used to give a location a certain look and feel.

prosthetic A fake part, made out of plastic or a similar material, used to make a person's face and body look different.

rehearsal An organized practice session before a live performance.

serial A series of actions where the acts are done one at a time.

FOR MORE INFORMATION

Halloween Haunt at Canada's Wonderland
9580 Jane Street
Vaughan, ON L6A 1S6
Canada
(905) 832-7000
Website: https://www.canadaswonderland.com
Halloween Haunt is one of Canada's largest seasonal haunts,
   housed in Canada's Wonderland theme park. Begun in
   2005, Halloween Haunt employs hundreds of people each
   season to play monsters, serve as maze guides, or other-
   wise work at three designated scare zones within the park.

Halloween Industry Association
2711 Centerville Road, Suite 400
Wilmington, DE 19808
Website: http://www.hiaonline.org
The Halloween Industry Association is a nonprofit trade organization. Its mission is to promote and celebrate the holiday through support of Halloween-related businesses in
   the United States.

Haunted Attraction Association
885 Stanford Avenue SW, #28015
   Grandville, MI 49418
(616) 439-4220
Website: http://hauntedattractionassociation.com
The Haunted Attraction Association's stated mission is to pro-
   tect, promote, and educate haunted attraction owners,
   vendors, workers, and enthusiasts.

Hauntworld Magazine
1525 South 8th Street
Saint Louis, MO 63104
(314) 504-3970
Website: http://www.hauntedhousemagazine.com
Hauntworld magazine provides information on building a
   haunted attraction, including current trends in the industry. Vendor links and a haunt forum are part of the publi-
   cation's online offerings. The magazine has subscribers
   worldwide.

WEBSITES

Because of the changing nature of Internet links, Rosen Publishing has developed an online list of websites related to the
subject of this book. This site is updated regularly. Please use
this link to access the list:

http://www.rosenlinks.com/RPFP/Haunt

FOR FURTHER READING

Allen, Kelly. *So You Want to Be a Haunt Entrepreneur*. Seattle, WA: Amazon Digital Services, 2011.

Bezdecheck, Bethany. *Acting*. New York, NY: Rosen Publishing, 2010.

Craig, Jonathan, and Bridget Light. *Special Effects Make-up Artist: The Coolest Jobs on the Planet*. Hampshire, England: Raintree, 2013.

Donahue, Tim, and Jim Patterson. *Theater Careers: A Realistic Guide*. Columbia, SC: University of South Carolina Press, 2012.

Henneberg, Susan. *Step-by-Step Guide to Effective Job Hunting and Career Preparedness*. New York, NY: Rosen Publishing, 2015.

Lau, Doretta. *Costumes and Makeup*. New York, NY: Rosen Publishing, 2010.

Mason, Helen. *Costume Designer*. New York, NY: Gareth Stevens, 2014.

Mayfield, Katherine. *Acting A to Z: The Young Person's Guide to a Stage or Screen Career*. New York, NY: Back Stage Books (Random House), 2010.

Mullins, Matt. *Special Effects Technician*. Ann Arbor, MI: Cherry Lake Publishing, 2012.

Pflugfelder, Bob, and Steve Hockensmith. *Nick and Tesla's Special Effects Spectacular: A Mystery with Animatronics, Alien Makeup, Camera Gear and Other Movie Magic You Can Make Yourself*. Philadelphia, PA: Quirk Books, 2015.

Rustad, Martha E. H. *How to Build Hair-Raising Haunted Houses*. Mankato, MN: Capstone Press, 2011.

BIBLIOGRAPHY

Associated Press. "Haunted House Business Getting Frightfully Hard." NBCNews.com. October 30, 2005. Retrieved April 4, 2015 (http://www.nbcnews.com/id/9855272/ns/business-small_business/t/haunted-house-business-getting-frightfully-hard/#.VQtc9OFczVI).

Chan, Siemond. "Producing the Ultimate Fright." Yahoo! Finance. October 17, 2012. Retrieved April 7, 2015 (http://finance.yahoo.com/news/interview-with-veteran-haunted-house-producer-steve-koppelman-20121017.html).

Louisville Halloween.com. "Danger Run—Includes 3 Haunts." October 2014. Retrieved April 2015 (http://www.louisville-halloween.com/danger-run).

MacDonald, Brady. "Why Don't Theme Parks Build More Year-Round Houses?" *Los Angeles Times*, October 7, 2014. Retrieved May 2015 (http://www.latimes.com/travel/theme-parks/la-trb-haunted-houses-yearround-20141007-story.html).

McKendry, Beckah. "The History of Haunted Houses." America Haunts.com. March 2014. Retrieved April 2015 (http://www.americahaunts.com/ah/2014/03/the-history-of-haunted-houses).

Occupational Outlook Handbook. "How to Become a Set or Exhibit Designer." April 2012. Retrieved May 7, 2015 (http://analyzemycareer.com/Careers/ooh/arts-and-design/set-and-exhibit-designers.htm#tab-4).

Occupational Outlook Handbook. "What Fashion Designers Do." January 2014. Retrieved May 2015(http://www.bls.gov/ooh/arts-and-design/fashion-designers.htm#tab-2).

Shawnee County Planning Department. Haunted house permit. Retrieved April 2015 (http://www.snco.us/planning/permitting_permits_hauntedhouse.asp).

Swedberg, Claire. "Terror Gets Personal at RFID-Equipped Haunted House." *RFID Journal*, August 2012. Retrieved May 2015 (http://www.rfidjournal.com/articles/view?9864).

Wainman, Laura. "Where to Celebrate Halloween in Washington: Haunted Houses, Scavenger Hunts and More." *Washingtonian*, October 2012. Retrieved May 2015 (http://www.washingtonian.com/blogs/afterhours/guides/where-to-celebrate-halloween-in-washington-haunted-houses-scavenger-hunts-and-more.php).

Wicentowski, Daniel. "So You Wanna Be a Zombie? One Day at Ghoul School." *Riverfront Times*, October 19, 2013. Retrieved May 7, 2015 (http://www.riverfronttimes.com/2013-10-19/news/darkness-ghoul-school-zombie-training/full).

INDEX

ABOUT THE AUTHOR

As a youngster, Jeanne Nagle briefly became a haunt entrepreneur—building elaborate haunts in her cousin's bedroom in the hopes of scaring the adults present. These days she works as a writer and editor. She has written a number of work-focused books for Rosen Publishing, including most recently *Careers in Internet Advertising and Marketing* and *Jump-Starting a Career in Health Information, Communication, and Record Keeping*.

PHOTO CREDITS